THE DRIVE FACTOR

THE DRIVE FACTOR

Getting Your Life In Gear For
The 7 Areas That Matter Most

RICK SARKISIAN, Ph.D.

LifeWork
PRESS

Illustrations by Jim Goold
Cover and Graphic Design by Riz Marsella

©2003 LifeWork Press
ISBN 0-9743962-0-6
Library of Congress Control Number: 2003110699
Printed in the United States of America

DEDICATION

To Joseph, the man closest to Christ.

ACKNOWLEDGEMENTS

With the always-present support of my wife, family and friends, I would also like to offer much gratitude for . . . the outstanding and insightful editorial contributions of "Bubba Mike" Phillips . . . manuscript review and many helpful suggestions from Ed Hurlbutt, Tim Drake, Christopher Knuffke, Johnnette Benkovic, and Louis Markert, Ph.D. . . . the encouragement of Steve Wood of *Family Life Center International* . . . the confidence of Kevin Dunn for applying the principles of **The Drive Factor** within his own family . . . the artistic skills of Jim Goold . . . the graphic design of Riz Marsella . . . and for the many others who provided assistance in turning ideas into words and words into the reality of a book.

TABLE OF CONTENTS

Preface

ARE YOU WILLING TO CHANGE?

There is only one person you must be with all the time — you. Is that person happy . . . at peace . . . satisfied with who you are and what you do? Or is that person in a state of turmoil . . . unsettled . . . edgy . . . constantly seeking happiness and acceptance? Are you trying to find a balance in your commitments between work and home? If you're willing to change, you're reading the right book!

My desire in *The Drive Factor* is to take you deep inside yourself — the only place to look for happiness or, at a deeper level, true *joy* in life. While we cannot change others or the circumstances in which we find ourselves, through God's grace we can change ourselves.

But how? By deciding to enter into a creative and dynamic partnership with God. When we make good moral choices and actions based on His guidance and direction, we *co-create* who we are and who we will become. The payoff is happiness and joy, every time.

God has provided the perfect plan for happiness — there is none better. To achieve real happiness and freedom, we need to discover the person of Jesus Christ. Why? Because we can't do it on our own. We are enslaved by sin, and we need to be rescued. Jesus is our rescuer. And His rescue plan requires that we do things God's way.

It was my original intention to write this book for all Christians, and it continues to be my hope that all believers will read and benefit from *The Drive Factor*. But after a great deal of prayer and reflection, it became obvious to me that this book would not truly reflect my heart unless it also spoke from my perspective as a Catholic. That's why, from time to time, you will find references to the abundant graces that flow from the Sacramental life in the Church *(like Confession and the Holy Eucharist)* and the blessings that proceed from devotions to Mary, Joseph and the Saints. If you are a fellow Catholic, you'll feel right at home in these pages. If you're a non-Catholic Christian, I think you'll still be blessed by *The Drive Factor*, since all Christians are united in their love for Jesus Christ and His promise of salvation. If you're "on the border" of Christian belief or perhaps following a different path altogether, I invite you to open your heart, mind and soul to the words offered here. They could change your life.

GOD IS CALLING . . . ARE YOU LISTENING?

What is God calling you to be and do with your life? If you're seeking a life of meaning and purpose, keep your spiritual "ears" open. God is calling you to a unique, personal vocation and mission — a particular way to follow Jesus designed just for you. Seeking God's call can help you discover your *vocation* (to *be* what God wants you to be) and your *mission* (to *do* what God wants you to do) in life.

Your **vocation** is made up of two parts: the **Universal Call** in baptism to live a holy life, and the **Specific Call** to a state of life, such as marriage, priesthood, consecrated religious life or the single life. Likewise, your **mission** is composed of two parts: the **General Witness** to others of Christ, and your **LifeWork Choices** — the specific use of God-given abilities to bring glory to Him in all things, whether you're a student, a parent, a worker, a retired person or at any stage in-between.

Discovering your personal vocation and mission isn't a single, once-and-for-all event. Rather, it is a gradual "unfolding" process, sort of like an apprenticeship that never ends as you continually learn more about yourself and your role in God's creation. Because of this, responding to God's call — striving to be and do what He wants — is a thread woven throughout the length and breadth of your life. For practical guidance in discovering your vocation and mission as you seek God's will for your life, see Appendix A at the end of this book.

WHO'S IN YOUR DRIVER'S SEAT?

Think of your life as the ultimate "road trip" — a spectacular adventure planned by God, who also provides everything you'll need for the journey. He built the roads. He drew the map. He even designed and built the "car" of your life with exactly the right features, the right power, the right color for your particular trip. Isn't it ridiculous to envy someone else's "car" designed for their journey, not yours?

Now, ordinarily when you drive your car, you know where you've come from and where you're going. But driving on God's road trip is different. On this trip, you wake up in a vehicle already in motion, clutching the steering wheel unsure of where you came from, where you are or where you're heading. It can be a frightening position in which to find yourself.

Fortunately, God has given you the ultimate navigator: *Jesus Christ*. And that means you have a choice about how you'll travel. Will you insist on controlling every aspect of your trip — from speed to steering — regardless of the Navigator's advice? Or will you faithfully follow Jesus' guidance, surrendering your will to accept the uniquely personal vocation and mission God has mapped out for you? You must decide.

If you travel like a "control freak," managing every part of your journey on your own, then success becomes your goal. To achieve that goal, you'll be faced with the daunting task of navigating your own car through the tangled highways and byways of change. When your only goal is the selfish pursuit of success, something very important is left by the wayside: love.

But if you're willing to give the perfect Navigator complete control over your journey, then love becomes a central

element. Love is allowed to freely express itself in the circumstances that surround you and in your responses to people and events. Life and love become thrilling and beautifully entwined, since neither can be fully controlled. You cannot "plan" to fall in

When you willingly follow God's map, true and lasting relationships occur . . .

love . . . it just happens. And that's when life takes on new excitement, meaning and joy!

It's really a matter of deciding whose map you'll follow. God's map is true and complete, encompassing the entire universe and the saga of salvation while still detailing your unique place in His plan.

But there are other maps you may be tempted to follow. If you're a rugged individualist, you may have created your own map — your own reality — and are traveling the rocky road of self-determination. Or perhaps you're the type that prefers to follow the shifting, sandy trails of modern culture, and are following a false map influenced by the mood of the moment. At best, these maps will get you sidetracked . . . at worst, they will get you hopelessly lost. *Whose map are you following?*

When you stubbornly follow your own map, other people become "things" to be used in your quest for success. When you willingly follow God's map, true and lasting relationships occur with those around you.

Belonging is a lifetime work.
It is our LifeWork.

If you truly desire to change, you need to see your life through God's eyes instead of your own. How do you do that? It starts by *abandoning* thinking that:

- ***Letting God be in charge of your life destroys your freedom.*** God wants us to be free. In fact, He *commands* it because the command to love is the command to be free. Love only exists in freedom, and cannot be forced. When we mold our will around God's will, we exercise our freedom in the most powerful way possible!

- ***It's enough to be a "good" person.*** That allows us to be defined simply by our culture and society. For true goodness, we choose no less than the Son of God, Jesus Christ, to reveal it to us.

- ***We will never really know if God truly exists or what He wants from us.*** We are real, the created world is real, and God is real. After all, He is at the source of all that has been created.

WE LONG TO BELONG.

If we understand that God has mapped out a unique road trip for us, with a specific vocation and mission for each individual driver on His freeway system, then we realize that each of us is part of His "master plan" for the universe. The greatest joy — the highest level of human happiness — is found in discovering where we fit into the flow of traffic in God's plan, and in belonging to Him. To belong is to be part of a community which defines our lives and becomes the core of why we are here.

Belonging is a lifetime work. It is our LifeWork. It is the use of all God has given us as we exercise our freedom with family, friends, co-workers, church members and society.

Those who don't care about God and His map for their journey are forced to travel recklessly, putting their lives together all by themselves. With no sense of belonging, they are on their own. They are "free," but only in the most superficial sense . . . like being free to clean the deck of a sinking ship.

If God created you *(and He did!)* then He would never abandon any part of His creation for even a split-second. It would be the cruelest of jokes for Him to do that. In His Word, God repeatedly assures us that He will never leave us or forsake us. Throughout Scripture, God teaches us that **happiness = belonging** and **belonging = happiness**. And when we choose to belong to God, then the more we will want to foster and pray for this special bond, and the more joyful we will become. **Simple!**

THE DRIVE FACTOR

A car goes nowhere without the driving force of its engine, properly fueled and transmitting its power to the wheels. This allows the car to move forward, and to deliver its passengers to their destination.

If the car represents your life, then *The Drive Factor* represents the driving force that propels you — the motivation and direction that you pursue in your life, based on internal desires and external forces. Driving a car illustrates this dynamic, as it results from both internal and external action. You are being driven by your internal functions of starting the engine, shifting into the correct gear, depressing the accelerator and moving the steering wheel. But you are also being driven by the car's external functions, through the proper operation of its engine, transmission, steering and braking system. Just as internal and external forces are involved in driving a car, they are also involved in driving your life. You can't always control the external forces that try to influence

your life. But you can decide to make God your internal driving force.

To bring about real change in your life, you must distinguish whether your driving force is God or the world—whether you are traveling according to His map or wandering aimlessly.

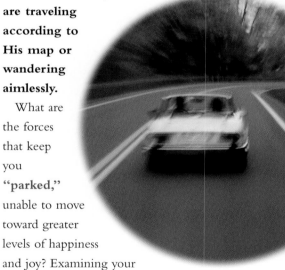

What are the forces that keep you **"parked,"** unable to move toward greater levels of happiness and joy? Examining your *Drive Factor* will help you decide whether you are driven by unregulated passion that can lead you anywhere, or by a **"spiritual guidance system"** which navigates your intentions and enables you to establish goals and targets. To see the difference, look more closely at the road trip God has prepared for you.

Get it in gear!

In order to break free from the world's forces that try to keep us parked, we need to listen to God and respond in grace. To do this, we must first understand how our lives fit into the grand scheme of things — our place in God's great freeway system.

It is a series of bustling super-highways and quiet country roads, efficient expressways and off-the-beaten-path scenic routes, all designed to allow everyone on earth to get to their destination. What is that destination? **When we follow God's map** for our lives, and entrust His Navigator with control of our journey, our ultimate destination is Heaven. However, those who refuse to heed the Navigator's direction, who stubbornly insist their own map is superior, who refuse to release their white-knuckle grip on the wheel, are driving headlong toward the most dismal destination in existence: Hell.

It's all about control. If I demand to control every inch of my life's journey, then I am operating without love. Love, after all, is not controlling. If I'm obsessed with control, I make it difficult for anyone to truly love me, and for me to truly love anyone else.

But God, in His greatness, allows me to **"leave the driving to Him"** — to relax and enjoy the ride with true freedom. Not the freedom to create new roads or redirect other drivers, but the freedom to fully devote myself to the journey and to enjoy the deep satisfaction that it brings. To carry "passengers" like love, generosity and truthfulness. To accept that God is God and I am not.

As rewarding as that freedom can be, we cannot be truly fulfilled travelers on life's road trip until we learn what it means to "belong." There are lots of ways to belong to others, some good and some bad. Slaves belong to their master, but few would argue that that kind of belonging is good. Success-oriented wealth-builders belong to their plans — another type of slavery. But others discover a deep sense of belonging built upon a lifelong partnership with God . . . a belonging that becomes evident through strong relationships and balance in the areas of life that matter most.

What about all the other drivers we encounter on life's journey? We are closely interconnected to them. Every person in our life has a different map to follow, yet they help us to define and fulfill our own journey as each of us seeks our unique place in God's plan. These other drivers — as well as the events and circumstances we encounter along the way — give relevance to our journey.

On every highway there are enormous tractor-trailers, miniscule motorcycles,

But in God's eyes, all vehicles — all lives — have equal importance.

dazzling luxury sedans, plain economy cars and other vehicles of every shape, size and description. It's tempting to think that larger, more impressive vehicles are somehow more important than smaller, more modest ones. But in God's eyes, all vehicles — all lives — have equal importance. If we don't see that, then our world view becomes too narrow and we look at life through the eyes of pride and judgment. Suddenly, the successful executive becomes far more impressive than the relapsed drug addict. The star athlete has greater value than the disabled child. That's not how the Creator intends His creation to be viewed. When we do, we deviate from the map He has created for us.

No doubt about it: God is truly a master **"Travel Agent,"** and has placed each of us precisely where we belong in His plan. Still, there are those who reject the road trip God has planned for them, and insist on driving their own route without His involvement. Much like building a house without a blueprint, the results are predictably disastrous.

Notice that God hasn't placed all of us on the same highway. He knows how tiring and tedious that would make the road trip of life. That's why He provides many off-ramps, interchanges and detours, allowing us to stop, stretch or simply enjoy

a change of scenery. These are decisions we are free to make in the course of our lives. When we make righteous and just decisions about life, God doesn't need to redirect us; after all, our trip will be filled with truth, beauty, goodness and supernatural joy — qualities that reveal the

. . . God reveals our vocation and mission as we journey through life making daily choices and decisions in the areas that matter most.

very nature of the master Travel Agent! But if we lie, steal, cheat or follow the path of anger or lust, then God is faced with having to make undesirable changes in our journey. We have misrepresented His nature. And since our road trip involves other drivers, our choices affect them as well, for better or worse.

If you've ever listened to jazz music, you've experienced this dynamic. Jazz is inherently improvisational and may, at times, sound as if each musician is playing independently of the group. Yet all must contribute to an overall sense of harmony and order for the tune to make musical sense.

As with all journeys, we can't see the entire route all at once. It is revealed to us, mile after mile, turn after turn. And that's exactly how God reveals our vocation and mission as we journey through life making daily choices and decisions in the areas that matter most. If you've read *The LifeWork Inventory* you're already familiar with the **7 LifeWork Areas** — the parts of every life that are the most important, and which must be lived in balance in order to achieve true joy and fulfillment. You'll learn more about the **7 *LifeWork Areas*** later in this book.

Perhaps the most daunting thing about seeing life as a road trip mapped out by God rather than a self-guided joyride is knowing that we can never simply "roll

We can't travel safely forward with our eyes fixed on the rear-view mirror.

back the odometer" of our past. Those events that are painful, humiliating or shameful remain forever a part of the journey of our lives. They're like the skid marks that remain as permanent reminders of a traffic accident or near-miss. But we can't travel safely forward with our eyes fixed on the rear-view mirror. With God's help, we can move forward without needing to erase or change the past. We can transform the *meaning* of the past and let events remain as they were, by letting God help us bring good out of evil.

Our trip along God's freeway system is the essence of adventure, with human freedom to make choices using our own will, and the divine freedom to either accept God's map or reject it. When we stray from His map by entering sin, God, through his mercy and forgiveness, can still restore us to our journey and make adjustments to the map, just as we may establish goals and from time to time make adjustments in how we go about achieving them.

PUTTING IT ALL TOGETHER.

So how does *The Drive Factor* . . . well . . . factor into the road trip of life? How does it direct the changes you desire to bring about? Your life, like any journey, has its share of twists and turns, detours and surprises. And it is ***The Drive Factor*** that propels you through these surprises as you pursue your interests, goals and dreams. ***The Drive Factor*** determines how satisfyingly you are both driving and driven through life.

But what's the force behind your ***Drive Factor***? Is it God, or is it the world? The distinction between them has life-changing significance. If God is removed from **The Drive Factor**, then by default you are forced to choose from the world's menu of superficial forces — things like success, wealth, power, pleasure and possessions. With God guiding your **Drive Factor,** you will always arrive at your target destination — true happiness, real joy, lasting fulfillment and deep satisfaction.

The choice is yours: listen to God and his personal call to you, or listen to the world and its shallow, impersonal promotion of values that make you less than you were intended to be. To truly change your life, you should be able to see the motivation behind your intentions, and whether you are following the voice of the enemy *(Satan)*. . . or yourself . . . or God. By seeking God's goodness and grace rather than the glossy attraction of the world, you have the right kind of fuel to power the drive and passion within you. Because human actions should always be preceded by God's grace.

Human *inter*action should be guided in the same way. Just as each vehicle on the

expressway is influenced by all the other cars, minivans, SUVs and trucks surrounding it, we need to recognize how others are driven and relate to them accordingly while staying true to the map God has drawn for us. **The Drive Factor** only makes sense in the context of God, where His grace allows us to shift out of **Park** (breaking the worldly forces and ambitions that try to hold us in place) and into **Drive**, where we can move forward while maintaining an eternal perspective. This means that we keep our eyes set on God, living out our vocation and mission as we head toward our ultimate destination: eternal life with Him.

When I introduced the concept of **The Drive Factor,** I asked you to think of your life as a car. Using the same metaphor, you can only find truth and meaning in life by using the right kind of "fuel" — grace that flows from prayer, Scripture, the Sacraments and spiritual knowledge — to give your life its proper "acceleration." Use something else for fuel and you may find yourself underpowered or stranded at roadside, falling far short of your destination and

The choice is yours: listen to God and his personal call to you, or listen to the world. . .

missing your opportunity for happiness, belonging and joy.

There are many other parallels that can help us see the car as a metaphor for life. In the car, as in life, we are both driven and driving: driven by the proper function of the car, while driving it to its destination. Along the journey, there will almost certainly be distractions *(worldly temptations, personal problems)*, potholes *(sinful pursuits)* and unexpected detours *(changing circumstances)* that need to be dealt with. Fortunately, the ultimate Navigator — **Jesus Christ** — remains ready at each moment in the journey to help you stay on course. He wants to participate in the mission and purpose designed for your life's journey. Are you yielding to the world's forces, or driving away from them toward Heaven? *You must decide.*

The 7 LifeWork Areas

I believe there are seven areas of life that matter most, each having its own degree of value depending on the choices we make and the lifestyle we embrace. Each day, we consciously or unconsciously allocate time to these areas; each day different from the one before. Whatever time is wasted cannot be

recaptured — we either use it well in these 7 areas, or use it poorly and waste it away. If you're truly willing to change your life, you'll need to get familiar with the following 7 *LifeWork Areas,* which we'll soon explore in detail:

1. Faith: Knowing that God is actively mapping a unique road trip for your life. *(Includes prayer, Scripture, Sacraments, grace and sanctification of time)*

2. Relationships: Getting to know your our own map as well as the maps of others. *(Includes parents, children, elderly, extended family, friendships, church, mentoring and counseling)*

3. Work: Understanding the purpose and function of the "vehicle" of your life. *(Includes occupation, volunteer activities and retirement)*

4. Knowledge: Learning how your "vehicle" works. *(Includes schooling, reading, media instruction, training and experience)*

5. Society: Helping other travelers along the way. *(Includes local community, country and world)*

6. Fitness: Keeping your "vehicle" in good running condition. *(Includes health of body, mind, emotions and spirit)*

7. Leisure: Taking occasional rest from the journey. *(Includes rest, travel, entertainment, hobbies and recreation)*

Your **LifeWork** includes all that you do in the *7 Areas* with the time God gives you on earth. Thus, your life is made up of much more than accomplishments in the workplace, classroom or home. It is through wise actions and balanced allocation of time, skills, personal qualities and interests in these key areas of daily life that help define who you are as a son or daughter of Christ. *"Balance"* among the *7 Areas* means not excelling in some areas at the expense of others.

PRACTICAL ADVICE AND CHALLENGING GOALS

The remainder of this book is devoted to exploring **The Drive Factor** in each of the *7 LifeWork Areas*. In keeping with our automotive theme, I'll introduce practical advice and challenging goals for each of the *7 Areas* using such familiar terminology as:

• **Destination** — Is the vehicle of your life heading toward your heavenly destination, or is it just motoring randomly from one situation to the next? Here you'll find guidance to help you adjust your steering and aim for your desired goals from an eternal perspective.

• **Fuel** — What's powering your car through the key decisions of your life? Fill 'er up with good advice here, in a simple-but-powerful "either-or" format.

• **Power** — Is your car humming down the highway? Or is it parked motionless in the garage, fully yielded to the earth's forces? These tips will ignite you to action, providing helpful ways to put your faith into practice in your everyday life.

• **Acceleration** — Ready to put the pedal to the metal? If so, here's what to expect — the "reaction" from taking proper action.

• **Under the Hood** — Time for a "tune-up"? Here you'll find specialized tools and practical ideas guaranteed to boost your performance!

• **Filling Stations** Practical Catholic advice for growing in holiness.

Ready? Start your engines!

CHAPTER 1

FAITH

Pursuing my lifelong passion for pre-war Fords often draws me to old car swap meets, a veritable feast for those looking for parts to complete their auto restoration projects. Usually staged in large outdoor venues like fairgrounds, these swap meets offer acres and acres of rusty fenders, flywheels and other body parts, always more junk than jewels. All browsed by hundreds of glassy-eyed men walking through the sea of discards as if in a daze, overwhelmed by the endless panorama of "stuff."

These auto parts are the discards of the material world. A wheel from an old Packard. A carburetor for a Studebaker Six. Door handles for a 1941 Chevrolet. Rusty, rotting, recycled or reproduced. It's all there.

What a stark reminder of how the things of this world pass away, but matters of truth and beauty — those elements that belong to God — never pass away. **The choice is clear:** you can place your confidence in the world's menu of possessions, power and position, or you can seek out those events, experiences and encounters that have eternal consequences, like passing your faith on to others.

FAITH
IS A GIFT
FROM GOD.

And thank Him that it is!

Otherwise our finite minds would never be able to understand the mystery that is God. So much of God is beyond our fund of knowledge and our capacity to com–

prehend tough questions like: "Why didn't God have a beginning? And how can heaven be eternal?"

Yet we have been given signs and clues that God is real. He is alive and He is enmeshed in our day-to-day existence. We can accept this at face value, just as we can accept the contents of a soup can by reading the label. We don't need to open it to believe that there's chicken broth inside. The label tells us so. And God has left us lots and lots of labels . . . Scripture, historical events, holy men and women who lived and died for their faith . . . all this and more so that we can believe with confidence in the One who made us.

■ ■ ■

DESTINATION
Thank God for the gift of faith
and pray that your capacity to believe, hope and know God grows ever stronger. Open your heart, mind and soul to nourish your faith through prayer, Scripture and the Sacramental life.

Believe in the unseen, the mystery of God. The more your faith increases, the more deeply you are able to believe. And the greater your capacity to receive His grace.

FAITH should be such an important part of our lives that it weaves itself through all the other **LifeWork Areas.**

FUEL
Prayer is the fuel needed to more deeply understand the mystery of God and strengthen your faith. Supporting your prayer life are all kinds of ways to study and learn about God: Scripture, Sacraments, the Catechism of the Catholic Church, spiritual books, audio and video resources, conferences, retreats, missions and pilgrimages.

Our daily walk with Christ is an opportunity for constant prayer, not just prayer once a day or when we "feel" like it. Pray while walking, driving and riding in planes, buses or elevators. You don't always need to have a formal prayer; just be open to God's presence. Invite Him into the moment.

POWER

You must decide to either actively seek God each day or passively keep Him in the shadows of your life. This requires a commitment to know, love and serve Him wherever you find yourself: at home, at church or in the world.

It is a matter of fully embracing Christ's kingship over your life or keeping Him as just a "concept" — to regularly talk with Him in daily moments of prayer, or just give Him the leftovers once the day's events are concluded.

ACCELERATION

With vibrant faith, time — our portal to eternity — becomes transformed each day. Time becomes holy. We no longer view the clock as our judge, but rather seek ways to transform time through Christ who is eternity in the flesh, and has entered into the world's humanity.

UNDER THE HOOD

Silence

Silence is the classroom of prayer. It is a place where God often speaks to our hearts, perhaps because we aren't talking so much. He commands us to **"Be still and know that I am God."** It may well be that He gave us two ears and one mouth in direct proportion to the way He wants us to use these senses!

Appointment with God

Beyond spending daily moments with God as events around us unfold, set aside a time and place specifically for entering into prayer. Make it the same time and place each day if possible. Protect and use this time as a way to go to the fountain and be refreshed by God's grace and guidance.

Transforming Time

Just as Christ has transformed time, so can we make time more holy, more sanctified. We accomplish this especially through prayer and worship because in some mystical way beyond our human comprehension, they enable us to "connect" with God's eternal presence. As we lift our voices to God in praise, thanks, petition and even sorrow, He hears us, and in this "connection" we dial into heaven.

We often are obsessed with the clock: "Did I do enough today or fail to manage my time properly? Was I industrious or lazy?" We allow the clock to be our judge and jury, making us feel good or bad about how we use time. We think of time as just another resource — something to be managed, parceled out and applied to our tasks. We read books about "time management" to help us prioritize each day.

We need to view time differently. Time is truly the gift of life itself. It needs to be sanctified, made holy. Use time to make the moments of your life opportunities to grow in holiness.

(See Appendix B for additional perspectives on the concept of time.)

Grace

To experience grace is to know the peace and joy that can only come from God. The more we know God and surrender our lives to Him, the greater our capacity to hold whatever graces we are worthy to receive. We are like an ever-expanding vessel as we grow in our capacity to love God.

When we have grace in our life, we experience true joy which is so much better, different and long-lasting than the passing experience of happiness (which depends on something "happening" in a desired way, otherwise we are "unhappy"). Notice there is no such word as "unjoy."

Stewardship

What God has given us, let us share with the world around us: our time, our talents and skills, our money and possessions. Give and give freely. Give abundantly. Find ways to share what you have in the church and the world.

Loving God

In every moment and every circumstance, seek what God wants you to do as an expression of your love for Him. Make wise choices, and live according to your choices, strengthened by daily prayer.

Priority No. 1

Faith is the most important area of our lives because it involves our relationship with God. As such, it has a dual role in the *7 LifeWork Areas*. Faith is both a stand-alone *LifeWork Area* and an integral aspect of the six other *LifeWork Areas*.

It would be incomplete to say that faith is number one without understanding how it must permeate all we do over the course of our lives.

Faith As Knowledge

While faith is a gift freely offered by God, it is also something that can be prepared for, fostered and expanded through study, Scripture, good books, reflection and philosophical inquiry.

Read Daily

Feed the soil that holds the roots of faith. You will grow stronger in your Christian life by doing so. Open up your Bible or Catechism.

Holy Rosary

Pray at least one decade per day, if not the entire Rosary. Remember, the *Rosary is not a tool — it's a weapon!*

FILLING STATION

HOLINESS IS THE EUCHARIST.

Does it feel like your faith is running on empty? Want to fill up on some high-octane faith? Who wouldn't? But that's not how God dispenses His gift of faith. Rather, the faith we receive at baptism is like a seed. When properly nurtured, the seed grows into something big and beautiful. On the other hand, if the seed is ignored or abused, it will never blossom into maturity.

If we sense a lack of faith in our life, there are many ways we can help it grow, while at the same time growing in holiness: through prayer and Scripture, through believing in the mystery of God, and most importantly, through the Mass and Holy Eucharist.

Jesus is here in all the tabernacles of the world, in all the consecrated hosts on all the altars of the Church. And when we receive Him in the form of consecrated bread and wine, we become living tabernacles ourselves. We hold the Son of God (literally!) within us and He becomes part of us.

The answer to holiness is in the person of Jesus Christ, who gives Himself to us in Word and Sacrament. Believe and receive. Go to the Eucharist in Mass and Adoration.

Practical Catholic advice for growing in holiness.

TREATING THE PEOPLE IN YOUR LIFE
AS FELLOW TRAVELERS ON GOD'S ROAD TRIP

CHAPTER 2

RELATIONSHIPS

The old, beat-up van in front of me had some writing on the back doors. Scripture, I assumed — something that would no doubt enhance my spiritual life through a freeway encounter pre-arranged by God Himself. I increased my speed so that I could pull alongside the van and read the passage that would surely have meaning for me on that day.

As it turned out, the message wasn't a Scripture passage. But it sure did have meaning for me . . . and still does:

NOT YOUR WAY
NOT MY WAY
BUT YAHWEH

In other words, God's way . . . God's plan. That needs to be our focus, rather than the plans we concoct for ourselves or those we adopt from the influence of others.

The path to meaningful relationships is paved with a desire to understand the God-given plans held by others in our lives. We must not only seek the unique map God has drawn for our own lives, but also the maps He has developed for those we love and care for. The more we get to know one another's maps, the more satisfying our relationships will be.

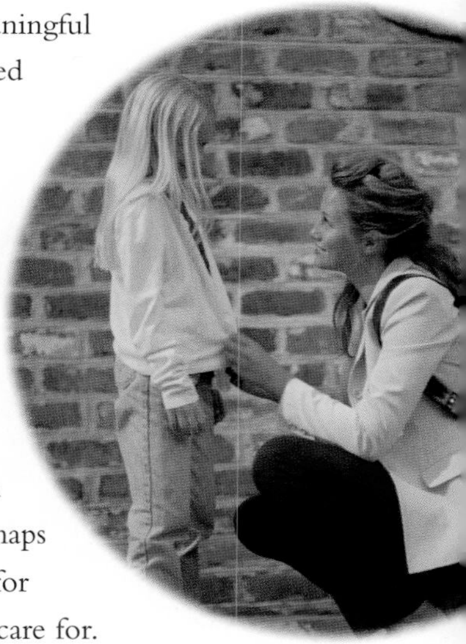

RELATIONSHIPS DRIVE OUR DECISIONS.

From birth to death, through all stages of our existence, our lives are filled with relationships. As children, our closest relationships are with our parents, brothers and sisters, extending to outside family members and friends.

As adults, our relationships become more varied: other families, aging parents, our own children.

And, in the autumn of our lives, our relationships still revolve around family, friends and fond memories.

So it is that we must consider the drive behind our actions, what makes us do what we do with others . . . what we say . . . what we feel . . . how we react.

■ ■ ■

DESTINATION

If we can view all others as equally important drivers in the journey of our lives, then we enhance our ability to grow in the hugely important virtues of humility and respect.

Rather than viewing ourselves as the center of the universe, we must view ourselves as motorists sharing the road with others who are following God's map for their lives. That makes us accountable to

Through fellowship with like-minded believers, God nurtures our sense of belonging as we live out the biblical command to "bear one another's burdens."

Him for all that we think, say and do . . . for touching the hearts and minds of others.

Our aim in life takes on eternal meaning because our actions affect others and affect how we proceed in the road trip of life.

If we are driven in the direction of power, prestige and possessions, then we are moving toward a worldly destination that is ever-elusive and only involves others to the extent that we gain from the interaction.

On the other hand, if we steer ourselves in the direction of humility and respect for others as we make the journey God has mapped out for us, then we experience the ever-present goodness and fruitfulness of His grace. Through fellowship with like-minded believers, God nurtures our sense of belonging as we live out the biblical command to *"bear one another's burdens."* The effects of these relationships extend far beyond our circle of fellowship, allowing God's love to penetrate the troubled world around us.

FUEL

You must decide whether you are going to have relationships that are not only filled with positive regard and respect for others, but also contribute to their well-being and personal needs.

If your relationships with others need improvement, then pray that God will provide you with the tools *(virtues)* you need to become a better spouse, parent, friend or relative.

With acts of kindness and thoughtfulness, the hearts and souls of others can be reached in powerful ways. From your perspective, make these actions ends in themselves, rather than seeking outcomes and rewards. Don't worry about results. After all, many of our good actions simply plant seeds in the lives of others and God takes it from there.

If you want to change the landscape of the relationships that surround you, first decide how important it is to do so. Ask yourself: what drives me now in my relationships? How do I view other people, whether they are part of my life or strangers? Do I want to have more solid and lasting relationships? What needs to change most in me?

It is a decision to reach out in love to those around you, cutting loose of your brokeness, your past disappointments, your lingering hurt and anger and your emotional baggage.

The alternative is to remain where you are, keeping up the status quo in how you talk, act and think, and in the way you treat others. You must decide. You must act.

POWER

In practice, view every single person as God's created wonder and as a fellow traveler in God's road trip. ***Do this every day.***

• **Ask** yourself what you can do to help this person to get to heaven.

• **Seek** improved relationships with difficult or unpleasant people. They are everywhere. They are in our families, in the workplace, at the grocery store.

• **Offer** help to others in need, whether you're asked to or not. Expand your view of the word "need" to include not just those with physical needs like shelter, food or clothing, but also those with moral or spiritual needs.

• **Pray** daily for the needs of others. God loves it when you do so, and the impact of your prayers will truly be felt by those around you.

ACCELERATION

Actions result in reactions. If you are driven to change the way you view others, then you ignite exciting new dimensions and greater depth in those you encounter. Not just those close to you, but even casual or coincidental relationships.

The payoff is a refreshing, grace-filled view of life from above "ground zero" and toward an eternal perspective that points you and others toward God's eternal kingdom.

 **UNDER THE HOOD**

Children

As parents, be driven to:

- **Protect** them from spiritual and physical harm.
- **Equip** them with the tools and skills necessary for adulthood.
- **Guide** them in making wise LifeWork choices.
- **Teach** them authentic manhood and womanhood.

> **WARNING**
> Failure to practice the above formula allows the world, in all its superficiality, to practice it for you. Ask Mary and Joseph to help you.

Choose Good Friends

Seek the company of those who are "driving in your direction" on life's road trip, regardless of where they are on the journey. Find those who seek goodness in life, and share your beliefs with them. As it says in Proverbs, iron sharpens iron.

Take Third Place

God first, others second, yourself third.

Humility

Commit yourself every day to growing in this paramount human virtue. The more humility you demonstrate, the more you take on the image of God.

Mentor

Look for opportunities to guide and counsel others, especially teenagers and young adults. Honor them with your caring. Drive yourself to find at least one person you can help.

Other Families

Do things with other families regularly. Visit them, camp with them, travel with them, have barbecues and meals together. *Pray together.*

Elderly

Be driven to connect with the elderly, not just those in your family, but the forgotten in rest homes and convalescent hospitals. Tap into their wisdom and life experiences and mirror God's love to them.

Mission Statement

Prepare a family mission statement that defines what your family is all about in God's view. How can your family reflect God's love in the home, the church and the community? *(For practical tips on helping you and your family draw closer to Christ, see my book, The Mission of the Catholic Family.)*

Wasting Time

Yes, I'm actually encouraging you to waste a little time . . . with a friend. Sometimes the best mark of a good friend is someone you can just hang out with, needing no particular purpose or event or agenda. *Don't forget family members!*

Seek Holiness

We can often discover holiness in the simple, ordinary tasks of life — rearranging a bookshelf, pruning trees, washing the car, making sandwiches. Great works are not essential for holiness.

FILLING STATION

HOLINESS IS A LOVING FAMILY LIFE.

Why is it that family life is often more challenging than anything else we face, yet is such a powerful means of drawing us closer to God and making us more holy? It must be that sometimes we have no choice but to trust in God to heal broken relationships within our family, dissipate anger, lift depression, bless marriages and equip our children with the tools needed for the adult world.

Isn't it remarkable that God chose a family as a way of bringing His Son into the world? And He specifically chose Mary and Joseph from all men and women to raise the Christ Child. The Holy Family, though certainly not without struggles — indeed, perhaps *because* of their struggles — is our model of family life.

Just look at the humility of Mary and Joseph, as well as their obedience to God's will. They were mutually dedicated to the interests of Jesus, and we, too, are called to follow their example. May we daily dedicate all we do to Jesus, praising and thanking Him for each event in our life (the good ones and bad ones alike), worshiping Him and reflecting His light into a dark world.

Before the birth of Jesus, Mary held the Word within her, and Joseph protected the Son of God from harm. Today, Mary still offers us safe refuge within her Immaculate Heart, and Joseph continues to protect us from spiritual harm. Mary's maternal love and Joseph's fatherly protection are powerful forces for all the ups and downs we encounter in family life.

Go to Mary and Joseph with your needs. You won't be ignored! They are there to protect, equip, guide and teach us, as they did Jesus, in all aspects of family life. Go to Mary and Joseph.

Practical Catholic advice for growing in holiness.

CHAPTER 3

WORK

The first car I owned was a fairly uninspiring green 1951 Chevrolet sedan. But when I sold it to purchase my second car, I was elevated into a position of prestige and prominence among my peers. For I was the proud owner of a 1957 Chevrolet 2-door hardtop. In tropical turquoise, no less!

But the initial monetary outlay was only the beginning of my investment in the Chevy. I spent the next two years striving to "improve" a car that was already considered to be top-of-the-line. I spent money on everything from a tachometer to traction bars, custom wheels to a Corvette engine. The more items I bought, the more items I felt the car needed. My '57 Chevy soon became a money pit on wheels.

Ultimately, I sold the car. It never ran all that well anyway. It overheated, idled roughly, often stalled, and rode like a tractor. No seller's remorse here — it was gone and good riddance. But I learned a valuable lesson.

I realized that if you mess too much with the factory-engineered original, you change the intent of the design and the architecture of something made to work well as-is.

In the world of work, we are also designed to function in the way God created us, using our talents to fulfill His mission in this life. When we try to change that design and "reinvent" ourselves, we tamper with the original work of God's Design and Engineering Department.

DON'T WORK TO LIVE . . . WORK TO LOVE.

Work is usually associated with our job, career or profession. It is often used to define who we are, especially for men. It is common to ask a new acquaintance, **"What do you do?"** Yet work as a single focus limits the possibilities for using our talents in the broader sense. Remember, work is just one part of our LifeWork, which involves all that we do with all we are given in the settings in which we find ourselves.

Truly, our lives are filled with "tasks" that could be defined as daily snapshots of work. These snapshots form puzzle-piece images that come together to reveal the big picture . . . the picture of our lives.

■ ■ ■

DESTINATION

Let's drastically change the way we look at work. Rather than seeing work as a means of economic gain *(or sometimes survival)*, reset your view of work as a daily expression of love for God.

How can you make that change? By acknowledging that all you have to offer the work world comes from God — your skills, talents, brainpower and physical competence. You offer Him thanks and express your love for God by being a productive, dependable and competent worker in your chosen profession. When you use your skills with this mindset, others see God's presence in the way you conduct yourself.

FUEL

You must discover where your skills and talents come from and how you can best use them. Did God as Creator give you certain skills, gifts and virtues . . . or are they just an accident?

If you believe that God has not only given you certain abilities, but also wants you to use them in a particular way, then keep reading. This book is definitely for you. If you don't believe this, then you'll face the lifelong challenge of trying to figure out the answers to life through the dice-roll of accidents and coincidences. In other words, you're on your own!

Fuel for a better understanding of your role in the workforce comes from acknowledging that:

> **All you have comes from God. He has a plan for your life.**

He wants you to use your skills and abilities wisely in all **7 *Life Work Areas***.

Work, in and of itself, can express the love and gratitude you have for God.

POWER

Place yourself in those settings that make the most use of your skills, and think bigger than your job, so that you can see daily opportunities to apply talents across all **7 *Life Work Areas***.

In practice, you are becoming a dynamic, living example of who God made you to be, because you are the image of the man or woman He created. . . sort of a package deal, because those who meet you see how you live out God's call in whatever setting you find yourself.

ACCELERATION

Once again, the landscape that surrounds your life will begin to change. Like a painting of the countryside, there will be more than the farmer's house in the picture. There will also be rolling hills,

vineyards, expansive sky, and so many more details that would otherwise be hidden from view. The world around you seems broader and larger than you noticed before.

This is because you have established a creative partnership with God. Your capacity to embrace life increases, and you realize that the narrow focus on **"job"** or **"career"** is limiting, compared with the wide-angle view of how you become involved in the **7 *Life Work Areas***.

More than ever, you can see how your life and your life's work fit into God's map for your life's journey, and you will dramatically improve your wise use of time as a precious gift from the One who created it. The moments of the day will flow by with a greater sense of calling, mission and purpose so that whatever you do *(or don't do)* becomes a matter of accountability for the role God has set aside for you in this world.

UNDER THE HOOD

Work Is Love

If your skills, talents and gifts truly come from God *(and they do!)*, then work is certainly the place to apply them and apply them well. By doing so, you express your love and gratitude to the God who made you.

Don't let your identity be defined by your work. Our work isn't really who we are; yet we often let work define who we are, as if what we do equals who we are. In reality, **who** you are becomes a matter of **whose** you are. Your identity is defined by answering two questions:

What does God want me to be?
What does God want me to do?

Go To Joseph

Seek St. Joseph, a great model of work and a powerful intercessor in matters of employment.

Laziness and Procrastination

Doing nothing can be a good thing, especially if it is a time for rest, recovery or silence.

Doing nothing as a response to unfinished tasks cuts against the grain of time being used wisely and well. Similarly, procrastination is normally the reaction to tasks that are boring, unpleasant, difficult or confusing. It puts off doing what needs to be done, yet days or weeks later, the task still needs to be done.

When trying to use the gift of time in wise and holy ways, procrastination is public enemy #1.

Volunteerism

Applying our personal qualities to people in need is another meaningful way to have greater depth in our lives. Life once again becomes bigger when we help others in need of food, clothing, shelter, cash, emotional support or spiritual comfort.

As Christ Himself observed, **"The harvest is rich, but the laborers are few."** Go into the vineyard and enjoy the satisfaction of helping others less fortunate than you. Give something back to the community as a way of saying thanks to God.

You say this sounds daunting? Then you're probably thinking that you'll have to make a major commitment or tackle some huge undertaking. Don't. **Start small. Build slowly.** That's how all habits become imbedded in our lives; after all, we're building new circuitry into our brains!

Seek at least one opportunity to volunteer your time in the next 30 days, then stay with it. There are plenty of options to choose from, like your parish, homeless shelters, food banks, handicapped settings, homes for the elderly and hospitals for children or adults.

Disorganization

Are you scattered and disorganized, zig-zagging from one activity to another just to get through it all? If so, then consider a simple and time-proven solution to the chaos and confusion that accompanies such days:

Take time each day to plan the next.

Spend just 5 minutes each evening planning the next day. Write down what you'll do and when you'll do it. Let this serve as your "personal trainer." A word of caution: refrain from planning your free time, even if you have lots of leisure activities in mind for a day off. It's easy to overdo it so that a free day seems like just another workday.

In other matters, such as dealing with clutter, saving too many items or surrounding yourself with too many possessions, begin using the trash can or give-away box aggressively to simplify, simplify, simplify. The less you have, the less you have to worry about. Less really is more!

The Meaning of Work

Work is a blend of skills, talents, gifts and interests, powered by **The Drive Factor** which gives us power and direction. What we do in the workplace should be consistent with a sense of personal calling, mission and purpose as we follow God's map for our lives.

Balance and Burnout

The theme song of the workaholic includes at least one verse that praises *"work for the sake of work"* and a refrain that asks repeatedly: *"what are you avoiding?"* These are tough issues that must be dealt with in order to properly ease out of the overload/ overwork syndrome.

Balance Illustrated

Imagine a large vessel full of water, representing a 24-hour day in your life. How will you use that water *(time)* to fill each of the cups representing the *7 LifeWork Areas*? Which cups will overflow, and which will remain bone dry? How can you more evenly distribute living water that sustains you and others each day? If you are working too much, try pouring some water into the cups labeled Relationships, Fitness and Leisure.

Balance helps to avoid burnout in any of the *7 LifeWork Areas*, but perhaps most often in the area of work. Too much of our time in one area causes neglect in other areas, and affords little margin or free time between them.

When we are overworked, over-loaded and overcommitted we find a decline in quality, enthusiasm, energy and interest in doing things well.

Balance is the antidote for burnout, and burnout is the expected outcome for the overworked.

7 ways to improve the quality of work.

1 Seek balance in life.

2 Conquer procrastination.

3 Plan and organize.

4 Apply skills and gifts competently and well.

5 See work as a component of a satisfying life, rather than its source of satisfaction.

6 Remember that work=love, not work=money.

7 Develop a sense of mission and purpose.

FILLING STATION

WORK DONE FOR LOVE IS HOLINESS.

Can work help us become more holy? It can, when we look at work the way Joseph did.

He was hand-picked from all men to join Mary in raising God's Son. What a guy! And a regular guy at that — a craftsman, wanting no more than to support his family, serve his God and work diligently at his trade.

Joseph is the patron saint of all workers, but he is much, much more. He is also known as the Pillar of Family Life and the Terror of Demons (*don't you just love that title?*).

A devotion to Saint Joseph opens the door to becoming equipped physically, mentally and spiritually for the work facing us. Not just the work involved in our occupation, but work in the home, the church and the world. Joseph is a most powerful intercessor and the greatest saint, second only to Mary. With her, he leads us to Jesus.

As a father, I know Joseph can be counted on to fill the voids I leave as husband, parent, friend and believer. He is there to provide unique tools for unique situations, and he teaches us that within work, we express love for those we support. When we follow Scripture and "go to Joseph," we cooperate with God's creative powers in the use of our skills, talents and gifts. Go to Saint Joseph, the Worker.

Practical Catholic advice for growing in holiness.

CHAPTER 4

KNOWLEDGE

In addition to being a self-proclaimed car nut, I have another confession to make: I love tools. There's just something about having workshop drawers filled with wrenches, sockets, pliers and power tools. And pegboards hung with mallets, hammers, files, saws and clamps. And what man's workshop would be complete without duct tape? *Lots of it.*

Of course, each tool has a particular function to perform. As I learned in high school auto shop, **"Use the right tool for the right job."** You can't change a spark plug with a tire iron and you can't drill holes with a socket wrench. So, knowledge of tools and how they work is as important as the actual skill in using them.

Think of God as the "Master Craftsman" who has a limitless supply of tools for getting us through life. Tools for

maintenance, breakdowns and repairs. Tools for raising children. Tools for the working world. Tools for the spiritual journey. Even tools to mend broken hearts.

God freely gives us all the tools we need. And just as important, He shows us how to use them. Each time we ask God for help in our struggles and concerns, we open the tool chest of our hearts and surrender to His unsurpassed knowledge of what we need and when we need it according to His will.

KNOWLEDGE DETERMINES OUR POINT OF VIEW.

Our perception of truth often begins with the quest for knowledge, for information, for ideas, for what we can learn about the world. I believe when that search is conducted honestly and earnestly, we reach the ultimate discovery that the only truth we can count on is what flows from the heart of God and the life of Jesus Christ.

What we know often determines how we think . . . how we assess the countless situations, large and small, that stream past us each day. What we think affects how we feel; the emotions that swell from our perception of events and people. Thoughts travel quickly from the head to the heart.

We are led to embrace knowledge that is good, and to reject all other information that comes our way in the dynamic flow of our lives. The adage, **"garbage in, garbage out,"** is more true today than ever before. What we soak up as "human sponges" can either be life-giving water or undiluted poison . . . or more commonly, water laced with poison.

■ ■ ■

DESTINATION

By seeing the value of knowledge as a means of expanding our awareness of the world, we gain increased depth to our lives. It's sort of like viewing life in 3-D instead of 2-D vision, and our love of knowledge brings about a love for the created world in which we live. Not a love for the world in a secular way, but in wonder of God's creative powers and our role in the reality He fashioned for us.

So we must readjust our view of knowledge as a means of learning more

about people, places and events, and look at these things from an eternal perspective. We learn to see everything from God's point of view, placed against the backdrop of His salvation and redemption.

FUEL

You must decide to either *passively receive* knowledge or *actively seek* it. To ignore the classroom of life, or hunger for it. You must ask, **"Does knowledge have value or does it just take up space on the bookshelves of the world?"** More importantly, consider how you can feed and nourish the empty spaces in your brain with the wondrous events of history, the issues that affect contemporary life and the wisdom that emerges from our search for truth.

Resetting our standards about knowledge requires us to seek it in the first place. All too often, we are inclined to receive passive entertainment from media events, athletic contests or non-productive activities rather than actively learning more about the world through sources of knowledge and information.

POWER

In practice, knowledge is sought from classrooms, books, magazines, television, audio/video programming, conferences, speakers and sacred Scripture and the Catechism.

Such information heightens our perceptions about life in general, from both a practical and philosophical standpoint. We learn about God and how world events conform or conflict with His mercy, love, forgiveness and creation. We are inevitably led to an eternal perspective and our sights are set on God and His heavenly kingdom.

Another practical by-product of our quest for knowledge is the desire to teach others what we know, sharing what we have learned from our life experience, the information we have received and the

wisdom we have gained. In a wonderful way, this process allows the teacher to also become the student; after all, so much of the educational process involves providing information, insight and ideas while listening to ourselves in the process. When you do this, you allow your mind to open more broadly to the possibility of even further insights about what you already know.

ACCELERATION

Ever-expanding knowledge about the world around us creates fertile ground for the virtue of wisdom. We actually become wise as we start seeing life from God's point of view. *What a payoff!* Just think about that — as you see your world, community, family and personal events from God's perspective, you create a seedbed for the growth of wisdom within you!

UNDER THE HOOD

Educare

This Latin term — from which we derive the English word "educate" — means to guide, to lead. It does not mean to teach, although most educators would consider themselves teachers. *Educare* connotes the idea of leading from one thing to another . . . from ignorance to knowledge . . . from darkness to light. Readjust your concept of education based on its Latin roots. You will then see yourself in a new way, as one who actively guides, leads, mentors, advises, counsels . . . in short, someone who can touch the hearts, minds and souls of others.

Lifelong Learning

Make learning a lifetime process. Seek new information and knowledge every day. Your brain can handle it. Like muscles, your mind needs regular exercise to stay fit. Experience is the architect of the brain.

Look for creative ways to gather knowledge beyond the traditional approaches that use printed material and media.

Intellectual Knowledge

Our intellect was created by God. When we nourish it with knowledge, we expand our capacity for confident existence in the world around us.

The more we know about the world, the more we know about the God who created it.

The Meaning of Life

Life is about knowing, loving and serving the God who made us. Doing His will in this world prepares us for experiencing complete joy in the next world.

Teaching the Faith

In order to teach, explain, defend or even understand our faith, we must first learn it. This means learning what we believe, and why we believe it; discovering the roots of our beliefs and how they are the foundation for how we view God. The best place to start: *The Catechism of the Catholic Church.*

Wisdom and the Spirit of God

Allowing the Holy Spirit to guide our thoughts and perceptions keeps us focused on our journey toward Heaven. Let the Spirit of God be your compass as you travel through daily life and absorb new learning.

There is no better way to maintain an eternal perspective than to surrender to the Holy Spirit each day to better see the meaning of life and continue the daily process of discovering God's will.

The Source of Knowledge

Scripture, the eternal Word of God, provides us with the most reliable source of truth in the world. In the Armenian culture from which I come, the word for Scripture means "Breath of God." As such, God can touch our hearts and souls through our mind using His word.

Passion

Are you passionate about something in life? Don't let knowledge quench that passion. Use knowledge as a means of looking deeper into what you're passionate about.

Why should you? Because the one, single passion that rises above all other passions, interests and pursuits has a spiritual dimension. It is the passion for God and his Son, Jesus Christ, enkindled by the Holy Spirit and the gift of faith offered freely to those who want it.

Deepening your passion for God may result in blessings like:

- **The light of God illuminating your life with untold grace**
- **The passion you have for other pursuits in this world taking on new meaning**
- **The will of God becoming more obvious with each passing day**

Beyond Scripture

Supplements to Scripture include the Catechism, devotional books, all kinds of audio and video resources, conferences, retreats, parish missions and pilgrimages. Look for the daily miracles all around us in nature, technology and human interaction. Beyond these things is the normal flow of knowledge from classrooms, newspapers, magazines, books, television and movies. However, much of the content flowing through the world's pipeline isn't fit for human consumption, so be careful what you choose.

FILLING STATION

HOLINESS IS KNOWLEDGE THAT BECOMES WISDOM.

What is truth? For thousands of years, that question has puzzled philosophers and fishermen alike. It was posed to Jesus by Pontius Pilate, and it continues to be asked today.

Unfortunately, this question seems to have led many to come up with their own version of the truth. With so many well-meaning folks basing their idea of "truth" on what they have personally known, seen or experienced, it shouldn't surprise us that there are wide variations in the definition of truth. If we want to become more holy, whose truth should we believe?

What we need is one truth to eliminate all the confusion out there. And we'll find it in Jesus Christ, the only person who ever claimed to be "the" truth . . . not simply "a" truth. He meant it. He proved it. And we can believe it.

The truth of Jesus is clearly revealed in Scripture, in the Tradition of the Catholic Church and in the teachings of the Magisterium. For a Catholic, the "tag team of truth" is composed of the Bible and the Catechism. Each clarifies the other. By reading both, your life will be immensely blessed — guaranteed — because you'll feed your mind on the truth, the knowledge and the wisdom of Christ and His Church. With the help of the Holy Spirit, they will infuse your heart and soul with a deeper, grace-filled understanding of the mystery of God and the spiritual life. So start reading! Go to God's revelation in Sacred Scripture and Tradition.

Practical Catholic advice for growing in holiness.

CHAPTER 5

SOCIETY

I once owned a Toyota Land Cruiser — 5,300 pounds of heavyweight SUV transportation. (Frankly, at that weight, there wasn't much "sport" in this sport utility vehicle!) On my frequent business trips, I would securely ensconce myself in the Land Cruiser's bank-vault enclosure of steel, and bully my way up and down the freeways of central California impervious to the dangers around me. Nothing could harm me; nothing could stop me.

Then one afternoon as I began a three-hour trip home from a meeting, I felt and heard a loud "thud" at 65 miles per hour. Within 20 seconds, there was no air in my left rear tire, the victim of foreign-object intrusion on the freeway. I was stranded on a narrow embankment of dirt, just off the highway. I was no longer invincible.

My Land Cruiser was paralyzed, powerless to protect me.

I got roadside assistance from an emergency worker and eventually resumed my trip home. Without his help, I would not have been able to get back on the freeway.

What a powerful reminder of how important it is to help others in need . . . those who are broken down, stranded or in need of repair. This episode illustrates how we also need the help of others in our own lives. We are all in this life together, and we are called to be the image and likeness of God to those we encounter daily . . . to be like Jesus to them.

WE ARE SURROUNDED BY NEED.

The hunger of the world isn't just satisfied with food, shelter or clothing. There is a deeper hunger — a poverty of spirit.

We must challenge our comfortable life and ask what we can do to fill the needs of others. Why? Because that's the way God wants it. It is abundantly clear from Scripture that Jesus was particularly concerned about the poor, and if that's the concern of Christ, then it needs to be our concern as well.

As obedient sons and daughters of God, we need to commit ourselves to pursuing the countless ways we can help others. To refuse is to reject the love God wants to extend, through us, to others.

■ ■ ■

DESTINATION

We normally see our local community as a source of comfort and acceptance, but we must also see it as a source of need. We should see the world not only for what it offers to us, but for what we can offer in return. By this healthy balance, we can help satisfy the needs of others according to God's will. We become light to those seeking the brilliance of God's love, even for those who don't realize how much they need God in their lives.

He lives in the hearts, minds and souls of the poor just as he does in the comfortable.

FUEL

You must decide if you want to live a self-centered life or a life that extends its branches, shade and fruitfulness to those in the world around you. It means going beyond your immediate frame of reference and familiar relationships, beyond your immediate family and friends, and stepping out of your comfort zone. It may take you to new frontiers and unfamiliar places. Yet God lives there too. He lives in the hearts, minds and souls of the poor just as he does in the comfortable. His love extends beyond church walls, and flows into taverns and homeless shelters. Don't turn away from the lowly and less fortunate in judgment, but engage them with the same compassion Jesus showed to the prostitute.

Is your life limited to **"self"**? Or is **"others"** a part of your vocabulary? Are you willing to give friends and strangers priority over your own needs by seeing how you can help them? You must decide.

POWER

Target the poor, whether the hunger is for food or faith. Within the next 60 seconds, you should be able to think of at least one local, church or world organization that you can assist in some way to reach the needy.

In practice, think about those in material poverty, and those who may be in spiritual or emotional poverty. Tap into your talents and gifts. Seek ways to help them. The blessings that accompany service to others will flow to them through you.

ACCELERATION

The rewards of helping others are truly gifts from God — they become part of the process of bearing fruit. He finds ways to bless those that extend the hand of help to others. You will experience great satisfaction in living an active faith, allowing God to use you as a vessel, pouring out His goodness to the world.

UNDER THE HOOD

The Rich

While much of our focus should be on relieving material poverty, we cannot overlook the materially-wealthy and realize that they may also have needs. Do you know someone in a middle- or upper-class position that is spiritually poor? *(We must be careful not to judge here.)* Pray about whether this is someone God wants you to help in growing closer to Him, and seeing God's love within you.

Planet Earth

To keep it all in perspective, view Heaven as our true home and Earth as a remote outpost. We live a temporary existence here, but all that we do on Earth has eternal consequences. The soul we touch today will affect other souls in future generations.

Pursue those things that will not pass away, that will remain when you are gone, like sharing the faith, spreading God's love and modeling virtues like humility and hope.

Service In Your Parish

Seek ways to become a part of parish life beyond Mass on Sunday. *Get involved!*

FILLING STATION

HOLINESS IS HELPING THE NEEEDY.

What's the "soundtrack" to your life's journey? In other words, what occupies your thoughts each day? Being "tuned in" to the world is like listening to AM radio, with its infinite number of "programs" to channel our thoughts. The station selections include such worldly fare as pleasure, possessions, prominence, self-praise, success and wealth-building.

But being "tuned in" to God is like listening to FM stereo, with its rich, static-free sound quality and positive "programs" that speak to our conscience, heart and mind. With God providing the soundtrack to our lives, we can see how our actions affect others. Which ought to lead us to be like Jesus to those around us, especially the poor. Right?

To become more holy, we must make a choice between AM and FM. We cannot listen to both at the same time. Fortunately, the Church has given us the examples of many saints who were "lifetime listeners" to FM. Saints whose missionary zeal met the hope and hunger of the unfortunate. Ordinary people who often accomplished extraordinary works, and did so only by the grace of God. What an inspiration!

Read about the life and times of a saint — there are lots of books out there. Apply what you learn. Remember the special regard Jesus held for the poor and downcast. Give generously to the community and world around you. And stay "tuned" to God's sound-track along your journey. Go to Christ present in the poor.

Practical Catholic advice for growing in holiness.

CHAPTER 6

FITNESS

My friend Bob had just installed a new transmission in his '63 Chevy, converting it from its original "3 on the tree" column shift to the infinitely cooler "4 on the floor" design.

One Friday night, he was showing his girlfriend how quickly he could shift while racing down the city's main drag. Attempting a "power shift" (applying full throttle while quickly tapping the clutch between shifts), a gear was missed and an ugly, grinding sound shrieked out of his transmission case. He had virtually destroyed his new 4-speed gearbox with the exception of one gear: reverse.

Bob spent the next 2 hours driving backwards across town to get his girlfriend home, taking side streets and trying to see the road by the dim illumination of his backup lights.

That's the night Bob discovered that his car had limitations, and that he had exceeded them. He was forced to choose an alternative method of travel — ironically, not only being forced to drive in reverse, but also with limited light, making it all the more difficult to see the road.

Like Bob's Chevy, we were designed to operate properly within a certain set of limitations. To operate at optimum efficiency and keep those limitations at bay, we need to maintain the health of body, mind and spirit. Poor fitness can prevent us from seeing the road ahead, and makes us only dimly aware of our progress. Ultimately, it can keep us from moving forward toward our eternal destination. Staying on course depends largely on staying fit.

SEEK FITNESS IN EVERY ASPECT OF LIFE.

Fitness doesn't apply only to your physical body. Yes, your body is out of shape when there is too little or too much weight, poor muscle tone or an unhealthy diet. But your mind can also be out of shape when it absorbs too little or too much information, or the wrong kind of information. And your spirit can be out of shape when you give in to temptation and sin, or when spiritual dehydration occurs due to a lack of the kind of food and drink that comes from living the spiritual life. Seek fitness in every dimension of your life.

■ ■ ■

DESTINATION

A healthy lifestyle for the body, mind and spirit *(and a healthy balance between them)* provides a rock-solid foundation for getting through life in good shape.

We often forget how closely integrated the body, mind and spirit really are; how they interact with each other. When the body feels pain, we have a mental reaction to it. When our mind is challenged by an unfortunate turn in events, we sense the effect on our spirit. And when we are spiritually hungry, our control of the body and mind is weakened.

Like everything else around us, the dimensions of body, mind and spirit are unique gifts of the One who created us. Just as God has mapped out a highly unique and personal journey for each of us, He has also given us the special combination of body, mind and spirit to provide the means for being what God wants us to be and doing what God wants us to do.

FUEL

You must decide between actively seeking a healthy lifestyle or staying just the way you are. Even if you are reasonably fit right now, there is a maintenance aspect of fitness that cannot be overlooked. A fit lifestyle is just that: a style of life that seeks health and fitness on a regular basis in the areas of body, mind and spirit.

Failure to pursue a fit lifestyle leads to bad habits and a decline in fitness. Think how easy it is to gain 5 pounds a year! *What kind of person do you truly want to be? Fit or flabby?*

POWER

• **For physical fitness:** Good diet and exercise. Simple.

• **For mental fitness:** Entertain good, positive thoughts, emotions and reactions to events, people and circumstances with an eternal perspective, dispelling the most invasive thoughts like anger, impurity, worry. Stop gossip, sarcasm, put-downs, name-calling and criticism of others.

• **For spiritual fitness:** Pray daily, read Scripture, think about God. Trust and hope in Him.

ACCELERATION

The payoff? Increased energy across the board — a stronger body, mind and spirit. A vibrant ability to penetrate the haze of the world around you, and more clearly see God in all things. What can be better than that?

UNDER THE HOOD

Emotional Fitness

Our emotions are closely related to what is going on in our mind and body. By having a strong spiritual foundation and the confidence that God is in control, we can diminish unhealthy reactions and over-reactions. In prayer, set the temperature of your "emotional thermostat" to determine the level of hot or cold that will emerge in the daily events you encounter and the people you meet.

Physical Fitness

Healthy food, regular exercise and an active lifestyle have so many bonuses it would be futile to attempt to cover them all here. Just go for it . . . do it . . . and if you don't have a healthy diet, get one. You know what to do and if you don't, there is plenty of advice on the bookshelves. If you don't know how — or how much — to exercise, get advice from your doctor, go to a personal trainer or read books on the subject.

Spiritual Fitness

The spiritual life must be fed regularly. We must go to the fountain of grace through regular prayer, study and worship to nourish who we are as sons and daughters of God. If we don't, we'll find ourselves parched and spiritually dry.

Sports

The athlete must develop self-discipline in order to perform well. We can learn from this. If self-discipline pays off on the playing field, it will also pay off in real life.

Children and Fitness

Getting kids involved with good food and regular exercise will plant the seeds of youthfulness that will continue growing long after they stop being young. Children's sports are a good introduction to a fit lifestyle, and help children learn the importance of a healthy balance between protein, fat and carbohydrates, and the value of cardio-aerobic exercise and muscle tone.

FILLING STATION

HOLINESS IS SACRAMENTAL CONFESSION.

I love lifting dumbbells. Why? Maybe it's the variety of exercises available, or the wide range of muscle groups that can benefit. Perhaps it's the simplicity of equipment involved, which helps me gradually train to lift heavier amounts and focus on specific areas like shoulders, biceps and triceps. But most of all, I like the fact that I'm mastering the weight, rather than allowing the weight to master me.

When you think about it, life can be seen as a daily "workout." The world is our gym. And we are challenged to gain mastery of our body, mind, spirit and emotions. When we fail — when we allow the world to master us — it's called sin.

In weightlifting, failure often results in physical injury. It can take time and medical attention before the body is free of pain and ready to resume its workout. In life, sin results in spiritual injury. Healing is obtained through the Sacrament of Confession.

Confession is not only a cleansing of our failings through Christ. It is a pipeline of grace channeled right where we need it for purity of thoughts, words and actions. Done regularly (at least monthly), Confession keeps us spiritually healthy and morally pure, allowing us to grow stronger in our ability to avoid sin. Go to be reconciled with the Father.

Practical Catholic advice for growing in holiness.

CHAPTER 7

LEISURE

I have held an interest in old cars since my youth. I began by drawing cars, then building models of them, progressing to restoring them, showing them and collecting a wide range of automobilia. Unfortunately, what started as a hobby later evolved into a grand obsession. Each day started and ended with a craving for more cars, more hard-to-find parts and more rare automobile literature. I bought and sold many classic vehicles, telling myself that each purchase would be a "keeper," only to eventually lose interest and replace that vehicle with another car-du-jour.

In short, I found that I was using my leisure time to succumb to the gravity of worldly possessions. It was all about accumulating material "things" rather than enjoying a rest and retreat from them.

A hobby can turn leisure time into a healthy, fulfilling thing. Or it can spin wildly out of control and dominate our leisure time with unhealthy obsessions and ambitions. How do you spend your leisure time?

LEISURE IS ABOUT LETTING GO.

Our pursuit of leisure is so strong that it often becomes our sole reward for hard work, for a job well done. We work, save and plan for all kinds of leisure activities, and spend much of our lives just thinking about them. Even the mere anticipation of leisure becomes a source of happiness! Well-channeled leisure affects us in all the other *LifeWork Areas*. In fact, we can successfully integrate leisure with faith, family, friends, fitness and even work.

. . .

DESTINATION

Like rest after exercise, leisure time allows for the recovery of our skills so we can use them again and again. We are refreshed, restored, renewed, and often find that leisure redirects our skills in new and exciting ways.

We need to reset our view of leisure in two ways:

• **First, see leisure as necessary, not just a place to park the leftovers of available time.**

• **Second, use leisure in ways that enhance our talents, rather than in ways that misuse or waste them.**

FUEL

You must decide whether to seek the good, the pure, the enriching in your leisure time, or seek activities that lead to temptation, sin, self-centeredness and self-indulgence. The menu of choices served up by the world typically involves more bad than good. We must choose between the wholesome and the garbage. There is barely any "gray area" or middle ground here. In matters of leisure, just ask yourself, "Would God approve?"

POWER

Approach leisure choices with these questions: Is this the best use of my time? Is this going to lead me in a good direction, or into a state of sin and separation from God? In practice, it is often the answers to these questions that determine whether the use of leisure time is good or not-so-good. Seek those activities that enrich all the other *LifeWork Areas.*

ACCELERATION

There is a direct and proportionate relationship between the quality of our leisure time and all the other *LifeWork Areas*. As we improve, increase and expand the leisure in our life, we find that the world around us gets bigger and brighter. As leisure is integrated into our LifeWork, it helps us use time more wisely. Leisure becomes an important and necessary element in our road trip of life.

UNDER THE HOOD

Entertainment

This is a big and confusing area for considering how to use our leisure time wisely. The entertainment world is overflowing with good and bad choices, more bad than good. We have to be very careful in choosing the movies and television we watch, the printed material we read and the events we attend.

Hobbies

Our hobbies can become so large a part of our lives that we become almost one-dimensional. We become our hobby. We *are* golf. We *are* a classic car. We *are* a quilt. There is one key word that must follow in the shadow of your hobbies: *balance*. Keep things in check. Watch out when your hobby begins to get out of hand in the areas of time, money and thoughts.

Travel

One of the best things you can do with your free time is "go somewhere." See more of the world around you. Experience other cultures — the food, the language, the people, the scenery, the history. This does much to increase your world view of God's creation and illuminate the needs of others less fortunate than us. Even a one-hour drive will have a positive effect. The benefits become multiplied by going even further to unfamiliar areas.

Rest

It is tempting to schedule our leisure time so that it is no longer "leisure" time, but "scheduled" time. Leisure time begins to feel like work. Use a portion of your leisure time doing nothing, just resting. No activities, no TV, no hobbies. Take a nap. Sit on the front porch. Recline and listen to music. It is in these times that God often speaks to our heart. Our body, mind and spirit have the opportunity to be refreshed and renewed.

Materialism

Ever find yourself obsessed with acquiring certain things, or spending lots of time thinking about what you want? We can easily be trapped into . . .

SEEKING THINGS THAT WE REALLY DON'T NEED . . .

WITH MONEY WE REALLY DON'T HAVE . . .

TO IMPRESS PEOPLE WE REALLY DON'T KNOW.

Remember the old *(yet still very true)* saying: **"You can't take it with you."**

FILLING STATION

HOLINESS IS IN THE ORDINARY.

Why do so many of us think of a vacation as a break from reality? Maybe vacation *is* reality! Consider this: by disconnecting ourselves from the workaday routine and separating ourselves from life's tasks, trials, traffic and trouble, we can see God without all the clutter and distractions that normally surround us. What's more real than that?

That's why I love leisure time. There is less to distract me from God. It's like cleaning the grime from a window, allowing me to see my Lord more clearly.

Of course, being human, we can all-too-easily clutter our leisure time with so many things — from events and entertainment to projects and puttering — that leisure is really not much different than work. Saint Joseph Marello, founder of the Oblates of Saint Joseph, spoke about "holiness in the ordinary" — drawing closer to God not through elaborate projects or lofty undertakings, but through the basic, mundane, ordinary tasks that make up everyday life. God is with us throughout our work time, family time — even our leisure time — and we should strive to "connect" with Him through our thoughts and prayers. Leisure is a true opportunity to engage in conversation with our Creator.

Prayer and Eucharistic adoration are choices we can make during our leisure time. They are a direct portal to eternity and the presence of God. They connect us to Christ. Quiet moments before the Tabernacle sanctify our leisure time and the graces we receive ripple into the rest of our day. And the Holy Rosary prayed daily becomes true weaponry to preserve our freedom from evil and draw closer to Mary. Go to Christ right now.

Practical Catholic advice for growing in holiness.

CONCLUSIONS

Actually, "Conclusions" is probably the wrong word here. Why? Because nothing is ending.

In fact, as you finish this book, you have arrived at the starting point of a lifetime of balance and living out God's will and purpose in the journey He has planned for you. In your desire to change your life, you can see that your LifeWork is not a once-and-for-all event, but rather a daily process of discovery.

We are each a unique, unrepeatable work of creation and an essential part of God's plan. If asked, God will provide all the tools and grace necessary for us to accomplish our mission and purpose in life. You must trust that He knows all of our needs and will respond to them.

I thank God for allowing us to cross paths in this way, as each of us pursues the road trip He has mapped out for us. I hope you have been encouraged. Now, let's pray that each of us will put these ideas into action . . . making every moment of our lives count for eternity . . . making sure we know what's driving us. May the "ride of our lives" take us to new, unexplored territories of true joy and purpose. *Ready?*

Appendix A

The Drive Factor is dedicated to changing the way you view your life — asking you to consider the best ways of using your skills, talents, virtues and interests to bring glory to God. Just as you are different and unique from every other person God has ever created, so are your personal vocation and mission, which have been custom-designed with your distinct personality and gifts in mind. By discovering your vocation and mission, you'll have the answer to the most fundamental question you will ever face:

WHAT DOES GOD WANT ME TO BE AND DO WITH MY LIFE?

That's the question most people spend a lifetime pursuing. Sadly, many never find the answer, and often go looking in lots of wrong places. But when you do find it, you'll experience the deep joy and satisfaction that come from knowing you are on the right path in life — the path that leads to eternal life with your Father in heaven. Think of your personal vocation and mission as your "road map" for that path — a unique travel plan that will take you to your ultimate destination: Heaven.

PERSONAL VOCATION

Your vocation is both *general* and *specific*.

General vocation

In baptism, to live a holy life in the Catholic Church, pure in body, mind and spirit.

Specific vocation

- **A calling to a state of life:** Single Person *(Pre-Vocation)* — Man or woman undecided or uncertain about their specific vocation and state of life.

- **Single Person** *(Called)* — Man or woman called to live a single, celibate life. May be a member of a Secular Institute, consecrated to a life of serving God. Vows include poverty, chastity and obedience, given privately rather than publicly.

- **Married Person** — Man or woman called to live in a covenant relationship with a spouse of the opposite sex.

- **Diocesan Priest** — Man serving a specific diocese with promises of chastity and obedience to the Bishop. Ministry in hospital, prison, campus, military or administrative settings may be assigned.

- **Religious Order Priest** — Man living in a community of other men with vows of poverty, chastity and obedience to his religious superiors and the Church. May work in parishes or be involved in teaching, missionary work, social work or chaplain assignments.

- **Religious Order Brother or Sister** — Man or woman living in a religious community with others, typically serving as teacher, nurse, counselor, social worker or administrator, or living a life of prayer. Vows include poverty, chastity and obedience.

- **Permanent Deacon** — Single or married man serving the church through the ordained diaconate, often in addition to a lay position held in the community. Assists priests and bishops in baptisms, marriages and preaching.

PERSONAL MISSION

Your **mission** gives you purpose in life, and is a means of bringing glory to God in all you do. Just like your vocation, you have a *general* and *specific* mission.

General mission

The Great Commission

(see Matthew 28) — sharing Christ with others in the world.

Specific mission

Your life's work - the specific use of your God-given skills, virtues, and spiritual gifts to bring glory to Him in *everything* you do and in all aspects of life; in your home, the church and the world.

THE PROCESS OF DISCOVERY

What is **your** vocation and mission?

There is no set formula or order in which you discover your specific vocation and mission. Everyone comes to that understanding in different ways and times. But the truth of Jesus' words — "I am the **way**, the **truth** and the **life**" — can be our assurance that He alone holds the only true road map for your journey through life and into the eternal presence of the Father.

1. Look for the Signs

God provides "road signs" along your journey to reveal His will. Some are **internal** as the Holy Spirit brings about feelings of peace when you are on the right track, or allows feelings of confusion when you wander off course.

Other signs are **external**, brought about through events, circumstances or settings around you, and through the counsel of family and friends.

2. Pray

Ask God to show you His will and plan for your life.

- The more you **pray**, the more you will **know** God.
- The more you **know** God, the more you will **discover** His plan.
- The more you **discover** God's plan, the more you will **trust** Him.
- The more you **trust** Him, the more you will **seek** His will.

So pray daily. Tell God about your day, and listen to Him in Scripture and the silence of your heart. As you come to understand your vocation and mission, ask God how you are to live them out. Trust God with all your needs and questions.

3. Use Your Talents and Gifts in the World Around You

Be active in your church and community. Do volunteer work. Help others. Show kindness every day. Just like trying on clothes, seek experiences to find out what "fits" best into your life. Start with service in your church.

ALWAYS SEEK

As you make choices concerning your personal vocation and mission, God will continue to reveal His will, helping you understand how He wants you to live out your call to serve Him. This is not a one-time discovery, but rather a lifelong revelation that unfolds layer by layer, year by year, as you live out your response to God's plan and seek the ever-present guidance of the Holy Spirit.

As I described in my book, *LifeWork – Finding Your Purpose in Life*, the Holy Spirit works in our lives the way sap works in a tree, bringing nourishment for growth as it flows up from the roots and trunk into the limbs and branches. The result? The tree bears fruit. And so do we.

Consider the vivid parable about the vine and branches *(John 15: 1-8)*, in which Jesus describes our lives as "branches" that abide in Him, drawing life from the vine and bearing fruit. Separate yourself from the vine and you separate yourself from life itself. Stay attached, and you'll become stronger and more deeply rooted through the Sacraments, prayer, Scripture, church teachings and the outpouring of God's grace.

Be assured that God calls you by name in a way that emphasizes your unique identity, setting you apart for a specific purpose in fulfillment of His great plan for the world. Are you willing to surrender your life to His Son, Jesus Christ? If so, He will be there to guide you throughout your life's journey — from highlights like employment, marriage, parenthood and retirement, as well as through difficult times, such as unemployment, widowhood, illness and disability. Ultimately, you will follow Him into death, crossing the threshold from time into eternity.

But that doesn't mean your life is on "cruise control." Rather, you are in a *cooperative* partnership with God, able to exercise free will while He remains present, interacting with you along the way. He helps you work out the details, and will be there to turn mistakes into goodness, and affirm right choices with a sense of joy and peace. It is not unusual for the "details" about your personal vocation and mission to be a great surprise — *and that makes the process of discovery all the more exciting!*

For a more comprehensive look at discovering your personal vocation and mission, I invite you to read my book: *LifeWork – Finding Your Purpose in Life* and view the companion video: *LifeWork – Finding God's Purpose for Your Life*. To explore God's mission and purpose for the family, I have written: *The Mission of the Catholic Family – On the Pathway to Heaven*. All of these resources are available from ***LifeWork Press***.

Appendix B

If *The Drive Factor* **were a movie,** this appendix would be the "cutting room floor" — where the editing process leaves stray bits and pieces of thought that don't fit into the main storyline, but which still may contain some viable ideas or worthwhile insights. Since **The Drive Factor** deals so extensively with the wise use of time, I included these "outtakes" which may prove to be helpful as you seek to commit every day, every moment, to the One who gives us the gift of time in the first place. That's the key to discovering the kind of *joy* that's deeper and more satisfying than anything you've experienced before! **Remember:**

To know *time* **is to know** *balance.*
To know *balance* **is to know** *peace.*
To know *peace* **is to know** *God.*
To know *God* **is to know** *joy.*

---

1. Consider the hourglass With or without God, the sand passes relentlessly until we are out of time.

2. The clock and the compass There is a relationship between time and direction — before we can use time wisely, we must get oriented in the right direction.

3. Where (and when) are we going? We are hurtling through space and time to an eternal destination.

4. It's a gift With each new day of life, God entrusts us with the remarkable gift of time.

5. Light your candle Once lit, a candle serves its intended purpose *(bringing light to a dark world)* until its light is used up. Unlit, the candle just sits there serving no purpose, merely taking up space.

6. A 3-way partnership An alliance is created when we become united with God and his gift of time — a partnership of man, God and time.

7. Distortion artist Satan seeks to distort our relationship with God by distorting time, tempting us to engage in the sinful or wasteful use of time.

8. Don't put it off To procrastinate is to say "no" to the wise use of time.

9. Most valuable virtue Humility is the key virtue for considering time and balance in the **7 *LifeWork Areas*.**

10. Not the end Death presents our life to God. Death is where time and eternity intersect.

11. Time flies Time is both reality and mystery. We all experience time in equal measure, but it seems to go faster as we age.

12. It's about time God transforms our time; He dispenses time in supernatural ways so that we can live it according to His will and purpose.

13. One way The best way to eternity is God's way.

14. The time, it is a-changin' Since Christ's arrival, the nature of time is different. It's no longer just a resource, it's now an encounter.

15. A timely answer The reason time exists? To help us trust God.

16. Don't be late Time is an encounter with eternity.

17. Moment by moment We make an act of trust with each moment of time.

18. Priceless The gift of time became more valuable when Christ entered into it.

19. Time trials Too often, time is a judge by which we evaluate how much we accomplish each day.

20. A liberating view With Christ, time has new meaning. We no longer need to fear failures, attacks or obstructions.

21. Inseparable Time has been infused with eternity.

22. No limits All the boundaries of time evaporate in eternity.

23. The time is now Eternity is here right now, enabling us to experience joy, peace and serenity.

24. Get busy Laziness mocks God.

25. Pregnant pause Our time on earth is a gestation period for our birth into heaven.

26. Lift your eyes If we try to dominate time ("I can do it on my own") or disregard it altogether ("I'm broken anyway, so who cares?"), we are taking a worldly view of time.

27. Breaking the bonds Christ liberates us from the tyranny of time.

28. First things first To understand time, we must understand Christ.

29. Time for a hug Let's use our time to embrace the eternal presence of God and the Holy Spirit that surrounds our life like the arms of a loving father surround his child.

30. The big question What's the best use of my time right now?

I would encourage your participation in *The LifeWork Inventory* that is also available from *LifeWork Press*. It will allow you to focus on your skills, gifts, virtues and interests, all within the context of *The Drive Factor* and the *7 LifeWork Areas*. It will also help you establish goals using an Action Planner and define your purpose in life by way of a Personal Mission Statement.

Art Credits